ROSE-BLOOM AT MY FINGERTIPS

Selected Poems
by
Rose Orlich

Rose-Bloom at My Fingertips

Rose Orlich

ADAMS PRESS
CHICAGO

Copyright © 1981 by Rose Orlich

Library of Congress Catalog Card Number: 80-68437
All Rights Reserved
Printed in the United States of America
First Edition
ISBN 0-9605036-0-9

Adams Press
30 West Washington Street
Chicago, Illinois 60602

For
my beloved parents
Stephen and Eva

Acknowledgments for First Printings

"Acrostic." In *A Concise Treasury of Tennessee and Kentucky Poets.*

"Complements."
"Praise for a Beautiful Woman."
"Rose-Bloom."
"Welcome Mystery." In *The Poet.*

"Doubly Dear."
"Window Scene." In *Our Sunday Visitor.*

"Shall I Know Thee?" In *Mountain View Digest.*

"One or Two." In *Poetry Today.*

Rose-Bloom at My Fingertips

Contents

Love	1
Rose-Bloom	2
Mila Mŏja	3
Love-Words	4
Communion	5
Missing You	6
Complements	7
One or Two	8
Enigma	9
Friendship in the Round	10
Surety	11
Whispers	12
Ambiguous Undulations	13
Joy	15
Praise for a Beautiful Woman	16
Light Lift	18
Summertime	19
Wood Anemones	20
Eden-Bird	21
Hearts-ease	22
Mind-Child	23
Losses	24
Words on the Wind	25
Window Scene	26
Mountain Laurel	27
Leaves, the Last: A Teacher's Blast	28
No Blanks, Please	29
Willfulness	30
Time	31
Twilight Trance	32
Passages	33
Queens of Quietude	34

Love's Mark	35
Midwinter Spring	36
Doubly Dear	38
Welcome Mystery	39
A Distraction at Study	40
A Temple Not Built with Hands	41
Reply	42
Flickerings	43
Walkers Past My Door	44
Variations on a Theme	45

Peace	47
Grave Thoughts at the Wake	48
Openings	49
A Swoop and Silence	50
Roots Clutch So	51
Insight	52
Yearnings	53
Dreams and Visions	54
The Teaching Major	55
Exchange	56
One Step Back	57
Recognition	58
Consideration	59
Acrostic	60
Shall I Know Thee?	61
My Gift	62

Love discovers the finest rose-being of the self.

Rose-Bloom

Rose petals, falling softly
From a fading, yet lovely rose,
Scent the world they fall in
From their opening to their close.

Petals, unpetalled, fallen,
Linger in sweetness there, where
A rose has known its fullness.
They incense a day of despair,

Make fragrant the fallen world
With its rose-being at its close
So that all may still know sweetness
Even after the death of the rose.

Mila Möja

We played that game so often—
"How much do you love me? A peck? A bushel? More?"
With hands held wide, I always claimed,
"The whole wide world could not contain love's score,"
And was rewarded with a charmed caress
That offered more than any world to bless
My swelling heart.
Oh, how I loved her,
Only she and I could guess!

And now she's gone.
I look beyond the grave
And seem again to hear her plaint.
"I'm old. You're young."
To which I always answered,
"*I'm* old. *You're* young."
"*Jâ sam stada. Tî si mláda.*"
And how I loved to hear
Surprised disclaimer to that grandiose claim.

Oh, could I now exchange my years for hers
And draw her from the grave,
To show a world of love,
I'd never even count it brave.

Love-Words

Be silent, love,
Marsh marigolds spring silently
From shadowed undergrowth
Of forests still—
Their golden gaze
A silent shout of glory in the maze.

Do not say love,
The orientals warn,
But let its blooms shoot forth
In golden ways
To prime the simple moments
Of a loved one's days—

A smile, a care, a flower sent—
Love's unvoiced voicing lifting to the light.

Communion

Sunlight shining through the window
Of your office, where we sat,
Silent and full of thought,
In the reading of a work in progress,
Drew your eyes to the loveliness
Of the tree-shaded campus, a green
Loveliness, holding the building
In which we had tried
To capture an artistry on paper.

You paused with me to share that outer sight,
As we together felt our hearts grow bright
And, every art, the shadow of that lovely light.

I loved you then and love you still
With the green light and with green will.

Missing You

Truly impoverished now, I say,
Bereft of your sweetness here today—
No gentle hand upon a door,
Fragrant smoke-screen or elfin lore,

No quizzing mind to call me to
Defense or challenge of a view,
No little gifts of charm and care—
Poem or picture, peach or pear.

Such poverty that does destroy
A little world made rich with joy,
Itself must find a richer mew
As I discover that I love you.

Complements

You brought a rose and I, a vase,
And lovingly we shared;
The two together took on grace,
No beauty spared.

You brought a thorn and I, a case,
And one did hold the other,
And so no hurt was there to brace
One soul against the other.

You brought a leaf and I, a flow
Of water, sustaining life;
Against that leaf the wind may blow,
But death escapes the strife.

One or Two

How many times I marvel at
The sympathy we two
Find in our separate actions,
Our ways in all we do,

As if our patterned notches,
Cut from the same bolt,
Were meant to match
And then complete

The separate-patterned piece.

Enigma

Don't tell me what I want to hear;
Tell me what is true,
And I will coast around those words
And love you.

Friendship in the Round

Heart's-darling,
What can there be
Between you and me
But only sympathy?

You read my mind
And kindly look
On all its convolutions
And every time you speak to me,

The earth takes note
And seems to stop its revolutions.
For universal harmony
Must claim its evolutions.

Surety

Tertius Lydgate of Middlemarch

My heart is a bird that has flown its nest
And come to another's heart to rest.
Nor will it return at my behest.

Love is a motion mysteriously made.
Who can know why the heart is obeyed,
When the head knows love must be delayed?

Whispers

No tide of my being
Can be still when your name
Draws the flood or the ebb—
Ineluctable claim.

When the flood is released,
The "Vibrato"—your hand—
Heart-rise toward your being
Races the sand.

When "Vibrato," silenced,
Issues no moving force,
The slightest remembrance
Gallops Neptune's seahorse.

A counter of reason
Cannot stay the flood;
Only finality
Can quiet the blood.

The currents of being
Flow without will
Restlessly, restlessly,
Still.

Ambiguous Undulations

At evening, casual flocks of pigeons make
Ambiguous undulations as they sink,
Downward to darkness, on extended wings. —Wallace Stevens

    Light going down into darkness
    Sets in my mind a fear
    That darkness will spread its hasty wings
    Over our little nest here
    Before I can tell a person revered
    What my heart sings.

    Sing in the daylight, my darling,
    The night will stifle your song.
    Sing in the daylight, my darling,
    The time is rushing along.

    And so I sing, my dearest,
    Of the joy you have brought to me,
    Of the beauty I see in your bearing,
    Of the strength you have to be
    The Great White Knight of the morning,
    Bringing light to my soul,
    The Great White Knight of the morning,
    Playing a prince's role
    In my world of darkness and light.

To live joyfully is truly to live, rose-bloom.

Praise for a Beautiful Woman

I knew a woman, lovely in her bones.—Theodore Roethke

Mama, you are so beautiful.

A child comes in.
Your eyes caress him with simple, shining love
As natural as the fold of a warm scarf.
You wrap him so gently in that kindly light
He is not even aware of its warmth enfolding.

Mama, you are so beautiful.

Someone has acted the proud and wronged one.
You have no bitterness to hold back;
Your being will not contain it.
Your love spills over
To wash out all envy, all hatred, all meanness.
You are so big—your small frame holds immensity.

Mama, you are so beautiful.

I bring someone home with me,
A person unknown to you.
You take her in—greet her with kindness
And never forget her
Because you take her in
To your home and your heart.

Mama, you are so beautiful.

Someone has sorrow, someone has need.
Wide-eyed, you follow the need of another.
You take it all in.
And in the taking, you give.

Mama, you are so beautiful.

You visit the graveyard
To pray for your husband, my father,

And your hands bless each grave you pass on the way.
Your love is so wide;
My heart is amazed.

Mama, you are so beautiful.

Light Lift

Suddenly a shaft of sunlight
    In a darkened room
Excites the spirit—
    Arresting gloom.

You, friend of light, though fond
    Of deepest shade,
Startle a sleeping joy
    From being-jade.

Light lifts the listless leaves
    Of plants declined,
As I am lifted by
    Your soul—sun-lined.

Summertime

Like a butterfly
With wings outspread
O'er a honeyed flower,
I flutter o'er your words,
Your voice, your gentle ways,
And draw from them
The healing power,
The grace of living,
The joy of loving,
In these short days.

Wood-Anemones

I saw the stars in a shadowed wood
Where none might hope to spy them.
Under my feet their pointed light
Scattered and dazzled in fragments white.

I had lost for the moment a childlike joy—
Had lost it, it seemed, forever—
When those points of light, those fragments of white
Rose to my sight in a lilt of delight,

Making the dark woods-world bright.

Eden-Bird

Such a rare bird—
Should I ever hope
To capture your bright plumage
In lines of ink?
Impossible to think—
Let me, on the brink
Of being, be content
To see that shape,
Savor its rich color,
Save its song,
And let it fly
In memory—long.

Hearts-ease

Oft have I known the joy
That bubbles from the heart in merry laughter
And clinging to the corners of the soul
Breaks but to form again in iridescent colors
That flood my mind with melody.

Oft have I known the grief
That importunes a graver melody
And riding on the gloomy might of unshed tears
Sounds but a dirge to my denuded years.
Heart-sighs have cried, to be born anew.

How then did wonder cross my path
And love carve out those tiny windows in the gloom
Where light shines in?
I hear the call of joy in all the lovely things of the world.
Beauty, brow-beaten by sorrow, I say, must ever lift
A brow, light-laden, in the moment of joy.

Mind-Child

A poem is man's wonder-child of mind—
        Less than divine—
At times a wayward imp, or yet, unkind—
A poem oft speaks from the reddest deep
Of the most secret heart almost asleep—
Demands that it be both heard and seen—
        Has to mean—
Cannot demean the words that it should raise—
Must make them mean in subtle, wingéd ways
More than alone the artless words unstirred.
A poem is like the song of rustled birds,
        But has to be
           Born—
      In the hush
          Of reverie.

Losses

A few poems bubbled out of me,
But I, looking at them with sharp eye,
Shattered them one by one
Into bursts of ephemeral figures.

And now they are gone,
Those pale, shimmering visions—
I have not the heart for revisions.

Words on the Wind

I have desired to be
A slim poet,
So slim may see
Some unity—

Words thrown away to the winds,
To keep slim
And beautiful
Words chosen—

Window Scene

Saucy little ground squirrel,
Flecked with white and brown,
You're the master of the square,
Peering from your hidden lair.

When the scene is quite serene,
How you dart about—
Choose the choicest bit of green
And at your banquet gaily preen.

Mountain Laurel

The way the wind blows up the leaves of gentle trees
To show their lacy underslips to all who care
To look upon these tumbled beauties
Must affront those nature gods who bear
A laurel image of the ravished fair.

Leaves, the Last: A Teacher's Blast

Because I've read a set of papers,
I feel inclined to do some capers—
Stamp my feet and juggle roses,
Take a few victorious poses.

"One set down and two to go!"
The challenge to my desk I throw—
Re-take my seat, glue-eyed by choice
And from the pen the red ink force.

"Freshmen, you'll have these on Monday!"—
I say, though it may be late Sunday.
The battle cry resounds in air,
As I slump lower in my chair.

No Blanks, Please

"My hobby, Sir, you say,
Should be listed, by the way?
It would add to all inducements
To entice a grant away?

It's awfully hard to formulate
In words that carry much great weight,
But if you think it will plans aid,
Then I must search for words as staid
As ever parson spoke to maid
And hope to coat with golden glaze
My one best hobby—just to laze."

Willfulness

Once upon a "would,"
I came to see
That "wish" and "will"
Can separate
Surprisingly.

I would wish will
Incomparably.

Time is the rose of life.
Time given is a petal scattered, a gift of life.

Twilight Trance

The world outside my window pane—
Lacy-fringed and leafed with light—
Has such delight for twilight eye,
I draw the shade reluctantly,
As if a newly-growing tree,
Fairy-like had beckoned me,
Cast a spell upon my mind
And lingered there beyond the blind.

My mind is flashing with the green
That is not now but yet has been,
Pointing my eye to sights unseen.

Passages

Two months ago we trod this wood
With wonder at the stars beneath our feet,
Cupped in the violet depths of sweetest wanderings—
Violet-strewn ways with wood anemones
To woo our antic gaze beyond recall;
There is no ending to the mind's remembering,
Though now we see a single flower over all
This lacy-shadowed loveliness of woods—
A white-edged growth upon a rock—
A stone grown velvet-covered with green moss—
And leaves that tease in patterns never-ending-new.
I kiss the world I stand in
Through your lips, your eyes, anew.

Queens of Quietude

Dusty among the tomes on my bookshelf,
They stand on rosewood pedestals—
Six of history's grandest women,
Whose dust so seemingly settled
Remains as unsettling now as then,
When they pursued noble or vainglorious dreams
To stamp their images on ages past.

I sigh for ancient glory such as theirs
But ring no bells to call them back,
Though each now stands
A bell-shaped figure, cast in bronze
And silver-kissed for shining surfaces—
The portrait bells—
I ring them not. My belles
Stand silent with potential sound
Ever ready to disturb the universe.

Isabella, Elizabeth, Mary, Catherine, the Maries,
You were not mute then nor will you be
When some braver soul than I
Releases your hidden melodies, or yet,
Disharmonies, upon an unsuspecting world,
Searing its soundless reveries.

Love's Mark

Memory of you creates a fortress-heart
Against all fears and all anxieties
That seek to storm my inmost being
With doubts and possible indignities.

My state of self is made so markedly secure,
Screams of mortality shrieking at the gate
Cannot destroy the spirit-wall you gave.
Death and despair and trouble and defeat

Range like the darkened spectres of the night,
None able to penetrate that crystallite
You built for me with all-enduring might
Of radiant, enchanting spirit bright.

Midwinter Spring

In memory of Karen Winter, a college co-ed, killed in
an auto accident

Magnolias in the spring are luscious blossoms,
Wide, white, sweet-smelling, full of fragrance,
Imparting a loveliness unparalleled in campus courtyard,
Transplanted from a Southern home
To frozen Indiana thawed in the springtime,
To a kind of green loveliness
That can such blossoms hold and cherish,
Though the warm season stays only a while.

So I had thought, as I looked out
The long, old-fashioned window of my room
And watched the delicate magnolia tree
Project its flowers, scattering white loveliness
Through an Indiana yard. Oh, beautiful full-blossomed
Magnolia tree, image of the deep South
And silent speaker of lost days of grace,
Repeated in this early flowering,
How could you hope to withstand a midwinter spring?

Sprung is all that loveliness, sprung forth
And wintered away. Only one glorious week
Until your petals blackened into ebony shadows—
And all that loveliness gone so soon.
Too soon brought forth—too soon denied.

So, too, this lovely white flower, fragrant in memory,
Bloom of a college, torn from the bough.
Sprung forth, sprung out, sprung into
Dazzling, flashing, dynamic space,
Ground in a car wreck—grounded and wrecked—
All loveliness gone.

Midwinter spring has its gladness.
And so her spring in the midwinter mildness
Held us in grace and gladness.
But the going of her, the passing of her,
The wilting of her proclaims
That winter is not dead. Nor shall it ever be.

My heart knows, though, that winter is not all.
Such grace must find its being somewhere,
Must be renewed in another spring, ever-springing.

Doubly Dear

Of all the dear ones in the world,
You are to me most dear.
Sweetly enshrined within my heart,
I keep you always near,
And pray that God may gently bless
My two dear ones—and with His love
Your souls caress;
And should I live a thousand years,
Still could I ne'er repay
What a loving Mother and a cherished Dad
Have strewn along the way.

Welcome Mystery

Suddenly in the greenhouse
She turned to me and smiled—
A stranger child, two years
Old at most—with rosebud arms
Outstretched, as if to gather
In my heart. Together down
The narrow orchard path we
Moved to childish prattle she
With her glistening eyes so
Gravely heard. 'Til suddenly
Again as with that first sweet
Rush and claim of arms outstretched,
Softly she brushed my cheek with
Gentle kiss as if to say
That we were similar kind.

That act still shines as
Sunlight in my mind.

A Distraction at Study

Shuffling, shuffling, shuffling
Down the long corridor of "home,"
You, dear lady, shelf-worn and fading,
Move into my mind
'Til Keats and Byron fade away,
And I am with you,
Shuffling through the hall of time,
And wondering then
How long the hall will be for me—
When I shall reach its end—
With what glad grace and gentle smile
Or sullen sombreness and sulky sadness
I will pass through.

A Temple Not Built with Hands

Time's finger has her forehead creased.
Care and Age, twin architects,
Have built within Time's space
A patterned, wrinkled face.
But Care did not destroy
Those temples of her eyes
Where heaven's blue yet shines
From fragile panes.
Age did not replace
The smiles of a thousand hearts,
Held in this one,
Nor leave undone
Aught that within could beautify—
Beauteous lines are woven still
By joy and love, by hope and fear—
Making this loveliness yet more dear.
The straightness of her ways,
Her glance reflects,
And though her body bends sometimes in pain,
Her spirit sings like the singing rain
Against a window pane.
She is quite radiant with the grace
Of an eternal place.

Reply

After a reading of Tennessee Williams's Glass Menagerie

"How is your menagerie?"
You asked and gaily smiled.
And I could not unfold to you
The thoughts that you beguiled.

Menagerie?—Yes, once the shelves
Were piled with china rare,
And should a choice piece chance to fall,
To me was black despair.

But that is now some years ago;
My shelves have since been stripped
Of fragile china—dainty shades—
With no perfection chipped.

Frail pieces still the shelves do fill.
But frailty, use has teased—
Perfection marred ev'n as dreams
Fading to realities.

And still the ware delights my care;
I value every mite.
A broken beauty can erase
The darkness from my sight.

Flickerings

A rose, a witch, a candle—
My three small gifts to you
Were brought to kindle friendship
Between us two.

The rose, a cardboard copy
Of what lay near your heart,
Bespoke my own heart's gladness
To share that part.

The witch, a little favor
Prepared for child's delight
For treat, not trick, desired,
Seemed a likely sprite.

A Christmas candle, blue-glassed,
And to be set ablaze,
Remained to my heart's sadness
Unlit for days.

Gifts doomed to the never-bright—
What makes a candle glow,
A witch delight,
And roses bloom?

Walkers Past My Door

They walk so heavily through life,
These women in their high-heeled shoes,
Stamping the pavement with high strife,
Walking as if they stamped the blues.

Feet, beating obsessions through the town—
Grim women, marching to dominant sound—
What burdens, I wonder, bear them down,
Grinding their soles against the ground?

Variations on a Theme

A "country lady" you called her—
Someone who had snubbed me time out of mind,
Because you noticed me
And were kind.

I could not see the "lady,"
Nor yet can I.
Can the country from the city
Be so far behind?

Or are we two, just you and I,
So far apart in courtly views
That to each other we can only be
A little blind?

Peace is the rose, wrought out of truth, thorny with trial, imbued with beauty.

Grave Thoughts at the Wake

This body, laid out so preciously in the bronze box,
Mocks my desire to spend a few more moments
With the woman I loved and cherished so mightily,
Though all are gathered for fine and final rites.

Eyes only for the face of that reclining figure,
I would give her everything there is yet to give—
Only the last full attention of my soul;
Toward her I am turned by this thought.

But her unmoving body moves my mind to see
Its padded part—only the packing left
From a beautiful spirit now set free.
She lives, my heart, yes, triumphs; I love her mightily.

Openings

Out of my pain came
The creation of a song.
Pain makes tender
What before was only strong.

A Swoop and Silence

One misty morning, propped against the pane,
Beneath a shattered circle of the glass,
Death met me at the window,
That would not let him pass—
A hawk whose fiery chase
Had hurled that single-minded bird
Through office glass.

Amazed, I gazed at
Feathered body squeezed between
A window frame and screen,
Thrust open by his powerful force—
The quiet corpse laid back
On feathered glassy bed,
Beak gaping still—

Capturing at last only the attention
Of a surprised professor
And the Biology Department,
The maintenance man,
A photographer—
The fury of the stilled bird's quest,
A silent moment of their gray imagining.

Roots Clutch So

Roots

    reaching underground to clutch at life
    through darkness and slimy terror,
    yielding not to the deathly stillness
    of unmoving quietude,
    of passive non-resistance

Clutch

    at my heart as I move through
    a town unknown to me, to see
    only the visible strangeness,
    terror at my heart, yielding
    to the life-urge—to root
    my transplant being in an eye-warmth
    Everyman discovers even in the darkness.

So

    to the light-song, to the heart-song,
    to the rhythm, to the blossoming,
    I reach.

Insight

Backward against the world I stood,
Pressed by a wall of mean hostility,
That flattened out my quaking heart—
Pinned me dimensionless
In a shrunken form.

"How can cries of the heart be heard
By those whose hearts are but words?"
My heart cried,
But inwardly I sighed,
For my heart, too, had become a word.

Yearnings

Where is the being lovely?
Eager mind will pray
To find that being lovely

Today.

To find that being lovely
Walking in this way,
One looks inside and outside

Each day.

For when he chances on this
Being lovely, say,
All the heavens open in

A magic way.

Dreams and Visions

O white-haired woman, spin your dreams
    Of past and future things
Upon that loom within your mind
    That every vision sings—

Its power, blazing moments, newly
    Spent in a dazzling whirl,
Endlessly spin the loom
    While experiences swirl.

Mind seeks to create an order
    From this rainbow vision of threads
First offering but motley color—
    Nothing bright wisdom breds.

Weaving, weaving, weaving,
    You with gray in your hair,
With red in your heart's own grieving,
    Seek the meaning and dare.

The Teaching Major

He was old, spoke too much and too loudly,
Grasping for youthful fire,
But finding only withered, charred remains
Of every stirred desire,
Unable to blaze forth.

Years had quickened hectic anxiety
For love, comfort, and joy
Ever denied in the
Seeking of one, who was
Old and alone, unwed,
Unpledged, uprooted ev'r.

Piling up things to take from one college
Dorm to another, he
Moved in pursuit of a
Vanishing dream, 'til one
Found dignity and stirred
A spirit-blaze of joy.

Exchange

"You see so little of me," I had said.
"And you judge so hardly
And remember so little
Of all the lovely moments
Shared in joy."

"But things taken away
Leave other gifts behind," I mused.
"For of a sudden a kindness
That has slumbered long
Wakens in soft smiles and ways
That might have withered
With your praise."

One Step Back

You said you did not love me
And what could I reply?—
Thinking of kisses sweetly given,
Of hands held and sweet words spoken,
Of a thousand conversations
Now passed by—
Did you lie?

Recognition

Love wakes the being;
I know that it is so.
Love wakes the being;
In love I wish to go.

I walk in hazes
Of many "musts" and "do's"—
Am lost in darksome mazes
Of close-kept private views.

But love wakes the being;
I know that it is so.
Love has waked my being;
In love I wish to go.

Those darksome mazes
Fill my heart with woe.
I see the loveless gazes
Of those that I should know.

Yet love wakes the being;
I know that it is so.
And love has waked my being;
In love then I must go.

Consideration

"Kind is love,"

I see proclaimed
On innumerable banners
Of gauzy fame,
And I,
While gazing at loverly lies,
Recoil from slogans
That hush my sighs.

Love is not kind
To the one who loves.
It is hard as the marble
That a tombstone makes
And cruel as time
That beauty shakes.

Every lover must come to grief,
Else his love will be but brief—
A strangled dove on a golden leaf.

Acrostic

Radiant He comes in the darkness
On wings of light newly living.
See how the world is brightened—
Emptiness filled with giving.

Over Him towers the heavens;
Radiance low He brings.
Love in a manger lowly,
In a bank of straw, sings
"Christmas joy to all mankind!"
Heaven-happiness springs.

Shall I Know Thee?

In the green garments of Eternity
I shall know my Love,
The God of heaven—
And shall love Him there
With love more pure
Than morning air
Or dew besprinkled
On earth's loveliest green.
My soul shall bend
Before His beauteous presence,
But He shall clasp this soul unto His own
And all Eternity shall stand
Breathless with desired Desire,
Poised in the green garments of Eternity.

My Gift

What have I to give,
O Babe of Bethlehem?—
Only my heart.
Such a little thing—
But loved by a little King.